corinna

corinna A-maying the Apocalypse

⋮ ⋮ ⋮

poems Darcie Dennigan

Fordham University Press New York 2008

Library of Congress Cataloging-in-Publication Data

Dennigan, Darcie.
    Corinna, a-Maying the Apocalypse / Darcie Dennigan—1st ed.
        p.   cm.—(Poets out loud)
      ISBN-13: 978-0-8232-2856-0 (alk. paper)
      ISBN-13: 978-0-8232-2857-7 (pbk. alk. paper)
      I. Title.

  PS3604.E5859C67   2008
  811'.6—dc22

                              2007049570

Printed in the United States of America
10 09 08 5 4 3 2 1
First edition

"Break, break, break . . ."

Alfred Lord Tennyson

Contents

Foreword *Alice Fulton*

Scientists at the Walters Art Museum are using spectral imaging to reveal the composite structure of the Archimedes palimpsest. Now the tenth-century Greek original of "On Floating Bodies," a text scraped and overwritten in the thirteenth century, glows red beneath a later black script. Darcie Dennigan's debut volume, *Corinna A-Maying the Apocalypse*, orchestrates its own spectral imaging in poems underwritten by lyric, narrative, pastoral, satire, and epic modes, poems whose lines are backlit by a numinous linguistic past.

In *City of God*, Augustine quotes Matthew: "Lay not up for yourselves treasures upon earth, where moth and rust doth corrupt, and where thieves break through and steal." In her poem "City of Gods," Dennigan obliquely responds: "I was a girl and a fleck of rust then. I was a girl and a poorly lit room. / On the roof, I was a clothesline thief trying on camisoles." She deflates patriarchal theology with a delicious insouciance: "The best god I ever saw is my mother named Betsy." And she declares her allegiance to local powers: "Just across the cosseted alley they sit: the gods in the dark, eating fishsticks." She is a poet of place, but her locations, like her locutions, are haunted by all they've *dis*placed. New Jersey during the 1977 blackout is palimpsested with Augustine's sacked Rome, and by two other apocalyptic sites: the pre-Columbian ruins of Mesoamerica Teotihuacan, "Place of the Gods," and Rio de Janeiro's *favelas,* made famous in the film *City of God.*

A palimpsest is a linguistic apocalypse: a devastation of text followed by an unveiling of text. The fabulously surprising sequence, "The Feeling of the World as a Bounded Whale Is the Mystical," evokes both the disastrous and revelatory implications of "apocalypse." "At kindergarten they must be having nuclear energy week," the speaker notes, looking at a child's drawing.

The radiation poison, she says, sits
inside the apple and the apple looks pretty. Then singsongs,

Bury the apple and bury the shovel that buried the apple
and put the apple-burier person in a closet forever.

We are both thinking *Then bury the burier.*
Both thinking of her picture with no people.

The sweetly caustic tone is characteristic, as is the fascination with recursiveness, infinite regressions that might be debacle or saving grace. "I would undo what I've undone," concludes "Interior Ghazal of a Lousy Girl." "We used gum to get out gum, / grease to remove grease," begins "I Sense a Second Heart." This wonderfully surprising poem celebrates the recuperative powers of the double. Like cancels like, and the resulting implosion just might be redemptive.

The mirror narratives of "Eleven Thousand and One" also keep faith with paradox and excess: "I didn't know exactly what I was doing there, so I was going / to do it harder." In this poem, girls doing shots in a Boston bar are prefigured by Saint Ursula and her eleven thousand virgins, sailing to their martyrdom. Artifacts of antiquity (an inscribed rock, bones, an arrow) and contemporary culture (torn wrapping paper, red ribbon, sucked lemon wedges) emblematize virginity across time and space. Robert Herrick's "Corinna Goes A-Maying," a poem of persuasion (some might say coercion), advises a virgin to honor the Mayday tradition of gathering greens and trysting in the woods. Dennigan's contemporary Corinna trysts with bygone and impending disasters. For her, rough winds do shake the darling buds of May.

I'm enormously grateful to Emily Rosko and Charity Ketz, brilliant young poets who screened the entries with scrupulous attention. They found many worthy manuscripts, but for me, Darcie Dennigan's poetry stood alone. There was nothing as idiosyncratic yet authoritative, as innovative and elegant, as untoward yet tender. I marveled at her poems' originality and was struck, quite forcefully, by their charm and depth. They had a quality of authenticity that can't be taught. Subsequent readings verified—and magnified—my initial response. *Corinna A-Maying the Apocalyse* drew me back to read again, a true test of the ineffable.

"The gods felt like / soft sootfall in my ears then. The world is never too much with us, / said the ash." I think the ash would know. Perhaps its uncanny life wish gives these poems their dismaying grace.

Acknowledgments

Thanks to Gabe Burnstein, and to my family.

Thanks to my writing friends and idols.

Thanks to Elisabeth Frost and the Poets Out Loud series, Fordham University Press, the Bread Loaf Writers' Conference, Byrdcliffe Artists' Guild, University of Michigan, and the editors and staff of the following publications, where versions of the poems in this manuscript appeared:

88: A Journal of Contemporary American Poetry
180 More: Extraordinary Poems for Every Day
The Atlantic Monthly
American Letters & Commentary
Barrow Street
Black Warrior Review
Combatives
Concher
Court Green
Forklift Ohio
Goodfoot
Gulf Coast
H_NGM_N
Indiana Review
jubilat
The Nation
Redivider
Salt Hill
Swink
Tin House

"The Feeling of the World as a Bounded Whale Is the Mystical" is for Erinn. This book is dedicated to my mother, Betsy Dennigan.

corinna

⋮ ⋮ ⋮

one

I Sense a Second Heart

We used gum to get out gum,
grease to remove grease.

With me this logic stuck—

when quiet got too much I put in earplugs
or hit the one I meant to clinch.

I think my mother survived eternity by drowning in its length.

Our sink was full of the eternity
of water, and I would wash

endlessly. Scum and skin dust heaped

on sheets, mouth spume on our pillowcases.
Water was drawn and drawn. Water quaffed

the dust's fine din. My househeart was—suffocating.

I saw—the way to feel my heartbeat was to beat it—
with pots and skillets, with umbrellas, with bullets—

I killed my heart to feel it.

Now I am one sodden bulk, one shot heart.
Still I am—in our dark yard. Measurelessly

aswim in the dark

beside a small girl playing hopscotch.
Her child thuds start the tide.

They start the cannonade—

The Virgins

My mother & her mother & hers,
on the porches of their white duplexes sit
sticking to their loveseats
& their calendars of pale days that cross
back & over the Pawtuxet River

to church, for last rites & births
& a Sunday nod to the marble Saint Mary.
The porcelain Mary three towns over
cries type O blood from her left eye.
Ladies come to her with daisies

& bouquets of Clytie's blood flowers.
The girl who loved Apollo stood still
by the cornstalks without sunglasses
following the sun for eons & hours
until her arms became petals & her eyes

one red pistil. Sit on your loveseat.
Mont Blanc hid its stigma in its tunnel,
in its tunnel a fire killed 39 travelers
crossing from Italy to France to
an explosion in the middle of snow.

See how the pale mountain sat
for the sun while in its heart
travelers burned, see how
I have gone from home to mythology
to the Alps & nobody has moved.

Love, when I say I want to be close
to you I should say more
about avalanches & bleeding out,
how we will move through eons
& hemispheres in a white clapboard house.

Eleven Thousand and One

There was this bar in Boston they were in.
It was October. The college boys had come back to town.
I was taking a walk when I saw them—five girls

singing "Happy Birthday"—"Happy Birthday to Ella."
Not that I could hear them through the window
from the street. Their singing was like wind through the high trees—

I didn't hear the sound—I saw it move across their lip gloss.
The day was Oct. 21st to be exact, feast of Saint Ursula
and Ella's birthday. The story goes that Saint Ursula died

a virgin. Ella probably would not. Ursula led 11,000
virgins to martyrdom. Ella led five girlfriends to a bar
on Beacon Hill. Whether or not anyone at the bar was still

a virgin was not something I could tell from the street.
It was a vagrant's twilight—clear, only just cool, and beds
of oak leaves all over the Common. Ella wore a black v-neck shirt

with a deep neckline. She seemed to feel exposed—she kept
her shoulders rounded for cover. Saint Ursula wore a tunic, I think.
She had no armor either. The other girls wore their shirts black and tight,

tight and black. They didn't really look like virgins.
Not to the college boys shooting darts in the back and squinting
at them under their Cocks, Bulls, Hornets hat brims.

Painters have made Ursula's face pale & resolute—
like a woman in a Titian portrait, only without the flush.
For flush, there were the girls, whose faces were blossoming

with lemon-drop shots—they'd lick the back of their hands,
sprinkle that little saliva patch with sugar, shoot down
a measure of gin, suck a lemon slice, then lap up the sugar.

Fun, though from a distance it looked—well, all that licking
in public—the sugar grits on their black shirts
nothing like stars over a black sea or the city on the suburb's

horizon—just a plain stain, a start of a girl's plain story.
The girls each did three shots in ten minutes. One was a little bigger
than the others. She did four shots, all elbows and gusto.

The eleven thousand virgins split up into three ships.
I don't know where all those girls came from. But they were going
to Rome. They had good wind & the going was fast, but

something happened. Ursula & her virgin army disembarked
in Cologne and smiled at men with dirty hands,
asking them to become Christians. And then an angel appeared

in the high trees, telling Ursula—someday, you'll die here,
you & all your tenderfoot friends—a message Ursula hid
in herself and so sailed on. Sailed on? I was leaning against a sapling's

thin, thin trunk. The face of each girl visible over the windowsill.
Each face bright against the bar's dark walls, but nothing like stars over
a black sea. I leaned against a sapling, but no angel appeared in the high trees.

Because it was October, the sapling was dying. Its leaves looked
beautiful—flushed and resolute. Only, hidden somewhere in itself—
maybe in its very thin trunk—was the secret that it was dying.

I didn't know exactly what I was doing there, so I was going
to do it harder. Ursula's face I made the color of wet concrete,
ashy, because of her secret, and because as I stood on the sidewalk,

it began to rain. Ella's face grew redder than ever—an almost
profane red. She was talking to the boys—challenging them
to a round of darts maybe, as one girl chewed her cuticles,

and the bigger girl laughed—it was a loud laugh, and a fake one—
I could tell. All five girls had secrets on their complexions.
It was a feast day of secrets. No one knew why Ursula's three ships returned

to Cologne. Why the prince of Cologne kissed Ursula's concrete cheek
and asked her to marry him. He was a pagan, a Hun. All the Hun men
wanted the virgins to sleep with them—on the ground, on beds

of oak leaves, I imagined. The virgins refused, and their blood
stained the leaves as they stared ahead, hard—at a god or the horizon.
The girls' mothers had told or hinted to them—never go down

on unfamiliar college boys in pub bathrooms. But then two of the boys
and two of the girls were gone. I should have prayed then for a god
to reveal her pattern. I didn't pray, though—I don't pray and what happens

is, sometimes, the sidewalk space beneath a neon bar sign seems to me
a holy station. So I lean against a dying sapling. In a chapel
outside Cologne sits a vault full of girls' bones. The arrow shot

through Ursula's throat by the prince of the Huns sits there too.
As Ella threw her darts, the cross hanging from a string of rosary beads
she wore as a belt around her jeans would sway side to side. Maybe that was

my imagination. All that's certain about Ursula is a Latin inscription,
ten lines by Clematius, etched into a rock. And then legend, and darkness.
There was something there about Ursula and her love of the faith.

And near annihilation: a fabulous heap of the gleaming pelvic bones
of virgins. But Ella lived in neither chaste nor epic days.
Ella loved only bright windows against dark streets. Or not—

that was more me. Ella was playing darts and doing shots. Sometime
after "Happy Birthday," after the bathroom groping, one dart went astray
and pegged her exposed collarbone. Then some of the boys went home

with some of the girls. One girl went home alone. The dart thrower
brought Ella to an ER for a tetanus shot, for a bandage,
for his love of the skin around her collarbone. Their artifacts: torn

wrapping paper; a thin, profanely red ribbon, scored and curled;
sucked lemon wedges. A waitress cleared it all away. For the love
of the faith of bright windows, I stayed outside, looking

for the pattern. Fact after girl after virgin fact. It had been
a vagrant's twilight. Now the streetlights were turning the sidewalks
into islands. Everything looked like stars over a black sea. Everything

seemed to be dying. From my holy station, I had kissed each artifact
and still did not see the secret. Then the bar shut down. Boston
had a curfew. Bright windows died early. After that, if you were still trying

to look in, you'd see just your reflection. I gave a halo to the sapling.
Made some girls saints and the alley, a black sea. Sorry mom, god,
you there, I said out loud, I need to make love to something.

The New Mothers

I got a job working in the orphan hospital. Mothers were all I thought about then. What mothers did, what you did if you didn't have one. Babies there never cried, not even the sickest of them, and that was not good, I thought. They did not cry because they got, somehow they got, that if they did, no one would comfort them. And I thought—I don't know why—someone should teach them about comfort. So the other nurses and I wrapped some clocks in blanket scraps. Each crib got a bundled clock. To mimic a heart. Like you do for dogs. That was the order of how we began to make mothers. We made them meter—the white noise of the clock beating in their sleep, or for one baby who had a brain disease and maybe couldn't hear, we thought, we gave him a loud clock, so he could feel through his mattress the beats. We set a pattern—a clock in the crib at nine o'clock was their nightheart.—They liked it. If we took it away, they would kind of fuss, and we'd put it right back, nestled in a blanket near their heads. I was happy we taught them a comfort. And the papers covered it—*a new invention from orphans' nurses—a babybalm device, a mother apparatus*—but really it was just meter, after all, just a pattern of beats—but the papers liked that too—that meter was portable—they thought it was cute that we were teaching the babies to say meter instead of mother. The words were so close in sound, and we were such suckers. We couldn't hold all the babies, and they were sick, but we taught them about beats and that was a comfort. But then the clocks began to break—they were just cheap windups—and when it got too quiet, the babies would fuss. We'd bought out all the clocks and watches at the drugstore down the street, and we couldn't hold all babies at once. Anyway, they wanted noise, not arms. So we began tapdancing and rhythmically whistling. We came on shift armed with metrical poems. We prayed for a tin roof and a heavy rain. And we were such suckers, we began to believe in the mothering of meter . . . me wearing my watch tight, much too tight, so that I could feel the beating against my wrist—it was a comfort—and as time passed and my wrist began to swell, another nurse asked, why so tight, like a tourniquet?—and I said, palpitating, *meter stops the bleeding*. At that time, I did have a real mother—most of us did. We'd been held. And now our own mothers were old and it was time for us to hold them, except they were far away, in other kinds of hospitals, and so we, pursuing the bodily pleasure of beating, pooled our money. We bought for the ward a grandfather clock, the kind with a large pendulum—we'd hold it on our breaks and listen. The papers reported it as *a sad turn of events*. We weren't supposed to believe in our own inventions. For *mother* now, we said meter. For *medicine*, we said meter. We taught the babies the Greek root—*med*, we said carefully, *to count and to care for*. See, we said in our baby voices, meter has always been a mother. No one else will love you, we said, in spite of time. We gave them the word and its sound and its feel so carefully, meting it out as a loving sentence. All that time the babies caged in their cribs. All those nights we'd beat on them, *say meter. Shush. Meter, shh, say meter. It's only your mother.*

Baby Girl Names

She will be Ona at the window, ironing a single white shirt in the dark.

She will be Augustine, dragging garbage down the driveway, curb, & city.

Put the baby girl outside, for the streetcleaner, for the can man.
If nobody comes for her, call her Maugra.

Lying in the yard, her head against the front stoop, she will be Bartlebia—

for her grandmother, who last night dragged her cans to the curb.
Who this morning begins again at the ironing board.

For garbage night again, when again a wrinkled shirt. She will be Bronaugh.
Time to hose down the gutters. She will be Udanadan over & over.

Give me back my mother in her white blouse & I will not begin again.

Else I will make her Pittie, Chimneysweep, Pillar of Salt.

City of Gods

Thistly Augustine, disser of the shy world, I cannot consider your city.
I cluck my tongue at sun & sky. The sky rises
too steeply. My soul goes no
higher than the highest highway billboard.

Oh Pericoli on a boat, a Mongoose, a motorcycle—you can't
draw the gods of New York from New Jersey.
Just across the cosseted alley they sit: the gods in the dark, eating fishsticks.

The best god I ever saw is my mother named Betsy.

Then-a-days, in the blackout of '77, from my roof I could feel
the gods sweating and moving. Some got trapped in elevators,
some got into black clothes & looted the glass-front stores.

No one was whispering Icarus! Phaethon! Glory glory golden!
I waited—to open my eyes and see my shy mother leaning over me.

I could feel dark stacked mortar, higher than the sun. I was great & complete
in that stack. The dark. The worldly world. The doth corrupt of Augustine
doth. I am corrupted by the beautiful sweating & moving.

Did you hear the divine shuffling across soft tar, the gods going
toward the girls sleeping out on the roof? The gods felt like
soft sootfall in my ears then. The world is never too much with us,
said the ash. Go back down into the dark rooms, said the ash,
ask Giovanna if her mother still loves me.

I was a girl and a fleck of rust then. I was a girl and a poorly lit room.
On the roof, I was a clothesline thief trying on camisoles,
graying camisoles hung out to dry between the antennae,
and a god in a window across the way would watch me.

Window dweller, god of spaces stacked with newspapers,
god of walks home from the N as the light ends,
if I ask you to turn my sooty camisole into wings and me into an industrial moth,
I am asking to be man-made—
I don't want to be too much more than ashes anymore.

Florid Gestures at Flo's Grille

On that night the waitress served watercress
while sobbing. Her customers sopped

thin crusts under the dichotomous moon. Oh,
her heavy black boots as she crossed

the kitchen. Oh, the flaught of her pizza-laden
arms. Across that night the unhalvable

distance opened wider. The watercress was cauliflower
diluted by tears. At the heaving bar

where no drifter's elbow touched another's, a locust
on a bottle rim made it halfway down to the gin

then half of that, & that,
then he drowned. All the glasses let

a salty drop. Apologies! I have no other
dimension for these people to live in.

Though she went from table to table,
the waitress was unmoved

by my fault. On that night I could call up only cheap food
& a sticky ground. All the mothers were faraway, &

the lovers. Jerkface, Jerkface,
Jerkface, bawled the waitress, the poor cur,

into a paper napkin. I should've fought against the distance—
the moon suddenly full

the waitress shouting Caress!
making vestibule love with the bouncer.

Only, as I looked in at all of them—
the bouncer's loose-necked gestures,

his girl with a throat of profound
phlegm—I believed (even still) more in this:

the back & forth,
her mop head across the spreading floor.

Starry-Eyed

The homeless man is in love with me.
I stand in his kissing distance, us breathing, the sky
ceasing and increasing. (Ours will be a brimful,
delicate, balancing-a-bowl-of-soup feeling.)
Don't they say commuters are the mothers of the homeless?
I must braid his hair, brush off his dust.
They say dust is the city's flour. I will make a dry bread
with his dirt. I would like to hold a crust to his lips. Would like
to lead him to a vacant lot. To say, *Sir*, then gesture, *This is yours.*
It's a house so large that comets wend in and out of its vents.

The homeless man is in love with me—ours will be a tiny and dirty
and shiny proximity. Doesn't he raise his hand as if to brush my cheek?
They say the riddles of time and space hide in the puddles
of a homeless man's face. I will be gentle. To see
what his eyes see of me. To be a picture a distant satellite seizes.
For him I will scour that lot with two hands, on one knee.
When our child is born and we find him sky-staring
we will say, that's our roof, our beams, our plaster and lighting.
Then my dreams will be his. Of lifting the metal roof off
a can of soup. Warming a puddle of broth under the stars.
In the satellite picture they will see—me
with a homeless man who stares with an intensity I take to mean
he is in love with me.
They will see my head mid-nod, me saying to this man, Please,
please—I can be as gentle as you want.

Sentimental Atom Smasher

So this guy walks into a bar and asks for a beer. Sorry,
    the bartender says, I only sell atom smashers

    And the guy says well isn't that America for you—
every happy-hour Nelson's a homemade physicist and no thank you,

just an ice cold one, but it's too late—suddenly, he's on his butt
    in a ballfield where handsome men are chasing a ball over grass

    sad grass, yellow like the hair of his once-young mother!
and again he says, no thank you—I've seen this movie before

And the bartender says it's a joke and you're inside its machine . . .

    Hey, the guy wants to say—I'm not *the* guy—I'm me
I'm just *a* guy who walked into a bar. I'm just a guy who retreats

to his car for a private cry. Instead he sniffs and cries out—
    The sky smells like the bologna from when I was a boy!

    Ahh, says the bartender, ahh yes. Someone has left
the refrigerator door of the cosmos open a crack

And the view! cries the guy. The beauty of an atom smasher,
    says the bartender, even from the cheap seats you see

    clear into 1952. And the guy, squinting into the distance,
starts to bawl. Maybe it's the vendors hawking

commemorative popcorn, or the programs promoting emotion
    ("the matter of the universe!") printed on material whose pulp

was milked from the trunk of a winesap apple tree, but—
    What's the matter? says the bartender. And the guy says,

I'm confused. Am I allowed to be homesick in a joke?
　　Yes, the bartender says. It's elemental, the bartender says—

　　How streets are downtrodden atoms and falling leaves are aflutter
atoms and beer is over-the-moon atoms. The moon's an atomizer

of all matter's perfumes: And the guy starts to parse it out—
　　Wait, I'm not smart, but if emotion's a material substance

　　then when a leaf falls in my lap and I hold it,
like an about-to-be-abandoned baby, I'm touching "aflutter" in 3-D?

　　Dear fluttering leaf!
Streets—I'm sorry for stepping on you! Apples—for coring you, and beer—

⋮　⋮　⋮

A guy walks into a bar,

—actually just the beer-drinking bleachers of a ballfield—and says
　　is this some kind of joke?

　　Well, says the bartender who has observed the little lamb
and the tyger burning bright and tickled their particulates,

because your life has lately been stagnant, we have yoked you
　　to a joke and we await the gasp that will gas up the cosmos . . .

　　Just then, there's a hit at the plate—and it's going,
it's going—gone to smash the guy in the skull

　　And since baseballs are made of nostalgia atoms, the guy,
with concussion, says I want to buy a coke for a nickel

　　I want to install apple pie perfumemakers in the crotch of every tree
Bartender, bring me dried nosegays! Start the stalwart pageants!

And the moon's spritzing its perfumes and the phlegm is thick and fast
And the bartender says time to wallow in byproducts:

Where we planted peanut shells, we got shaky, palsied trees
Where we planted nickel cokes, we got nicked cans

Where we planted baseballs we grew large, sad eyeballs
        as we watched for something to grow. Still, still

        we atom-probe: In a dark building a child is
about to be born. The smell of bread is about to

        break. And our guy is going, O spring evenings!
How I used to stand yelping in the alley by the bakery . . .

        Who are these boys throwing baseballs? Who is this baby?
O bartender, tell me, what is the message in this light rain?

But the bartender's dark eyes are flying
        over centerfield, over the rooftops and watertowers of the joke's

        universe, over alleys and cold valleys of refrigerator light
toward an aptest eve where these street kids are hurling a ball into

        the moonlight and the moonlight is curdling into freon . . .

two

The Feeling of the World As a Bounded Whale Is the Mystical

The child affixes one of her little pictures to my refrigerator.
She asks, Can you detect the radiation?

There is a house, one tree, and grass in dark slashes. A sun
shining. Beneath, in her child letters, she has written *Chernobyl*.

At kindergarten they must be having nuclear energy week.

One could look at the picture and say everything is in order.
No, I say, I cannot see the radiation.

The radiation poison, she says, sits
inside the apple and the apple looks pretty. Then singsongs,

Bury the apple and bury the shovel that buried the apple
and put the apple-burier person in a closet forever.

We are both thinking *Then bury the burier*.
Both thinking of her picture with no people.

The poison sits inside the people and the people
still look pretty, she says. Still, she says, sweetly, Away with them.

The child is not a flincher, which is why I love to tell her stories:

Of the poisonous man who tumbled into the cold sea
and turned the sea poignant.
His bones glowed in the cold deep like dying coral.
His ribcage was a cave for small, lost fish.
Flecks of his glowing skin joined with green algae
on the sea surface, where, on a boat, his widow choked
as she looked down the sun shaft for her husband's greening body.

What is sunlight through seawater most like
but the strange green fire
that burnt the man?
—Who had worked atop a steel hill until a whale—
a great green whale—bumped into the continental shelf
and the steel hill cracked and its poison leaked out.
And the man began to melt . . .

What I am jealous of in the child, what I really detest in her
is how she nods

with kindergarten grace and finality. Primly, into her pinafore,
she tucks what I've told of the story.

On the refrigerator her picture looks so pretty.
There is no end to the green or pollen or the feeling of the bees coming.

Or of a hill and sky of poison.

On fire, the man working on the reactor must have looked wavy—
like a man trying to ride a humpback through the fast green sea.

Her picture on the refrigerator looks so pretty.

When I wake her from her nap I will ask
if the dark green slashes are meant to be
radiance, not plain grass.

⋮ ⋮ ⋮

The child asks, What can keep me safe?

We are riding in the car. She has seatbelt
across her lap, her shoulders, her gut.

She is little so she has seatbelt across her forehead.

It is a long ride, a good time for the plane crash story.

She is driving. She feels safer when she drives
and this allows me room to gesture expansively

about the plane taking off, the plane going down.

"No," he said, defiantly.

It was the man who sat in the plane as he drowned.
"No," he said, "No." Except he said this in his head.

Fine, the child interrupts. I will not ride in planes.

Wrong, I say. It's tiresome to repeat the same adages,
but that's what you do with children:

For when there was a plague inside the houses, the people slept on the roofs.
What was that but sleeping on the whale's back?

And the stars made a whale in the sky and the grass
shone so brightly in the starlight that the night had a greenish hue.
And with the night whale shining down—

He who slept on the roof died on the roof, the child finishes.

It was the story of the ballplayer I was trying to tell.
Flying rice to earthquake victims and his plane stalled over the sea . . .

Before the plane went down the man saw the four corners of his fate:
rice paddy where the lethal bulk of the last bag of rice grew
grass on his first ballfield
moss on the rock where he sat while his son was being born
green dial on the control panel—

And the man who saw this saw the green whale, the child finishes again.
She is curt when she is scared.

Why I let a small child drive my car—

well, this child knows my feelings on safety.
If we only stay careful and awake—if we are good people—

Ha. Then nothing.

And the child
asking her question. Her quavering. Hope against hope. Child voice against adult.

We drive, avoiding highways
where a beautiful green slippery beast sits trapped behind the wheel of a car

speeding toward a sea dock—when there's nothing but desert around.

. . .
. . .

The child calls me on my cell phone to ask, What is fate?

It is late. I imagine: the child on the couch curled up.
That grief has made her

smaller. Her cheek in the curve of her phone.
I whisper over the line *A beautiful green whale rolled over in the sea.*

He saw the whole sky in one blink and then he saw through *the sky, his eye was so big.*

I imagine: the child rolling her eyes.

He cried whale tears—

The child interrupts, Why? Because he had seen the limits of the world, I say.

The child says, That whale's a fathead.

I ask, Do you want to know why whales have fat heads?
No, the child says, I want to know what fate is.

I have never believed in a sky beyond the sky, but the child has.

When she believed—it was water she could drink.
For me it is like a jelly jar after the last drop of water has dried.

What to say about a whale whose eyes saw the boundaries—
now this curl in the world? This well in the water?

The child has always been smarter than I. And surer.
Meanly, I have waited for a night call like this.

And so the beautiful green whale left home to live
where the lip of the water eats
the light of the moon.

I imagine: the child scowling.

Forget it,
she says. And then, indulgently, You can tell me what whale tears are like.

Poor green whale, I could have said, with significance,
bound ever after to look only within himself.

And if the child asked the right question, I might have said, Wait.
Wait, the abridgement of *whale's fate*.

But the child is scared and I am scared so
I say, Whale tears? They're the mothersoul of honeysuckles.
Diaphanous elephant ears.

The child has had a parent die. When she asks, Will I die?
I say, Where are you? And she says very smally, I don't know.

Both our phones sweaty in our hands.

Are you crying, she says.
I say, Wear, wear, wear.

It is advice. It is the abridgement of *whale tear*.

Then comes the story—who is telling whom?—
about how I would have comforted her, if we lived in the same house.

How I would have padded downstairs to her on the couch
and put the house phone back in its cradle.

How we both would have stepped outside into the small yard of a green night
to take fistfuls of bright grass, crushing the stems

to form the curves of a whale
as the green juice leaked through our knuckles.

And though I knew it would ruin her, I would say to the child,
You be the yard and I'll be its grass.

You be the sky and I'll be its gas.
You be the whale and I'll be its fence.

How near morning, the child, again her clear-eyed self,
would have asked, What are we doing?

And I said, Child, let's last.

three

⋮ ⋮ ⋮

Arearea

In July in a large room with late afternoon light & fat electric lamps & those of us in Grand Central's
open space, I asked.

Left to right we had our face
in our hands. If we leaned in

we would hear not the yappers or sadshoe scuffers but our own teeth, grinding, & a child, biting
an ashy streetstand apple.

The moon did not love us
though we were full, though we were

a thin yawn at times. Mother, we said, motherless, less & less. With a fist of lilies of the valley
from the gravel valley streetstand.

Happiness hated us because we knew
it was not the sun but small

as a vacant chair's slight heat & we had to get up, for tickets, for a look at this room's gold clock
or the Sky Ceiling's winter

constellations, stained from us
breathing our yellow breath.

What Were We? Where Were We Going? When Could We Jump In The Fountain? In rooms on rows
on our way to trains

by gate, by platform, we fit.
We'd come from bed.

If old, our afternoon skin sallowed as we pet the cat in his box. If young, we chased the stray pigeon.
I asked about bigness,

one of us lying down
on our suitcase, head back

to the Sky Ceiling. I asked about joyousness, all of us very small, we with our one spindly finger counting fifty-nine bright stars,

two fish & one goat
in the firmament.

Within the tableau the moon was our face with black curtains pulled all around it.

Tallies & Sentinels

Salt
was not always so cheap. The woman

who lived here before tasted it only twice—

once in cake & once at the corner
of Crossen & Main when her baby in lace

died. Then she put the salt in its cellar

& with a sponge wiped it from her face. Then she
died. Others came, had their losses & meals, made

gardens & sadness. They ripped lettuce for salad.

They died. With long arms around their pillows they
had practiced their hacking & weeping for when

they died. I can see them, the couples who lived here

before—something about their pillows & the doorjamb.
I see them as I rip lettuce for salad,

as the blue moon over Jericho trickles over

our supper, our lettuce & moon lasting
so long until we make the room a bedroom, & sleep.

We are at the start, about to put salt upon salt

& I am sad at what a little stab our bed lamp makes
in Jericho's large nights. We'll start with our long arms

looped then turn them around our pillows, split.

To our bedroom screen the sleepwalkers come: the woman
who keeps between her breasts a black sponge,

the pietà without her son's bones who hunts a body

to fill her arms, & before dawn, the archaeologists who
dig our bed for graveyards. If they've gone when

we wake, I will scratch a tallymark on our bedboard

each dawn until the bedboard breaks. Then with our hands
we'll make more losses & meals, between our hands we'll

hold the warm bedroom lamp until I remember how once

a lamp exploded in a woman's hand. So supper, & sleeps,
garden & lamps & then. Then suddenly our pillows are

a long rain of down feathers. Our bedroom screen, sill,

the doorjamb—they break in half with a snap & I can see
clear across—I will have been watching the other

women watch. They bend their elbows on their sills & see

me making marks. A line for the day with cake, a line for
yesterday, two more, then a slash across. We began

dulcetly, in raptus, to trumpets. Then silence, little

& hard, guttered the streets. The woman who lived here before
had miraculous habits—making socks, then wearing them through

then sewing holes without imagining the asphodelian

heel, the next hole she was making. She will not
tell me how to disbelieve the end. I'll practice waking

to wrap bedsheets around the morning. I'll put long arms

around the room as if it were mine. Then I'll dream
the woman said salt, salt, salt. I knew how all this will happen

but forgot. So trumpets, & cake, miraculous habits

& gutters & then, then I can put it off only so long.
I knew how this would happen but forgot in the trumpeting

as we began in Jericho. It will start to be off-limits

to us now, though we had a down garden here & in our sleep,
under a blue slat of moon, we would loop & split.

We died. Even as the women in Jericho were saying how

there'll always be a Jericho, we died. You see how
it makes me alone to know how this will work as I rip

lettuce for our salad, but if I make meals anyway,

in large nights, in graveyards & do not say what I've seen
then what's, what's the pity?

Grand Central Terminal

1913, the girlghost died here in a gas explosion.

That eavesdropper, that lamenter, that moonface,
she begs the late-night ticket seller to measure her home.

I knew the area—Heaven was one hundred and twenty-five feet high.
World was fifteen levels of tunnel & track.
Time was twelve hands on a thirteen-foot face.

The girlghost—I dreamed she kissed me in the Kissing Gallery.
She shined my luggy shoes with her handkerchief,
light impact, how do you do, heartsease.

For the Fortunato brothers who lost their fruit stand,
the redcap who knelt to pray on the tracks,
for the ones in the waiting room with lunette windows
who love to look at the moon,
she sang a gubbinal—
and then the light fell short & the people gasped.

I heard her last in the Whispering Gallery—
I said ladder, she said ellipse.
I said I wear an eyelet skirt, she, moiré patterns.
Omissions, I said. What came out of her mouth: pearl.

The immortals, said the girlghost, we are
as like as milk to milk.

After the Station Fire

Tonight this place, The Station, is gone, lost to a
devastating fire, and so are at least 96 of its patrons . . .
in a town of 30,000 best known for what it once was
than what it now is.
—New York Times, *February 22, 2003*

The town's got a ghost named Misericordia.
My Serene Cordelia. Miss Air Accordia. (just) Miss.

In my yard, my dark yard, statues of girl saints
and arbor Marys whisper *Ave Maria. Misericordia.*

Some are born to sweet delight. Pipefitters slip
under pipes. Machinists knit themselves in the tool & die.

Miss sears her core, her face and dress and form,
in a fire in a bar. Let me go around again: some are born

to sweet delight. But if hard is holy, ashbit
from her fire is a splinter of saint's bone.

To be hard is to be dead, a mill of misbegotten
wheels, and I love the wretches, the pugilists,

the bar waitress named Misericordia. Who hasn't drunk
holy water against the flames? Who hasn't inhaled gas fumes

to fan them?—To unlock the tin box of Misericordia's
mysteries, find her mist, her corsages. And kiss the tin for

its hardness. Miss My Sweet Cordelia. The pipefitters sing
of a bar fire, how the bar's a squat box and it's no mystery

how the wretches died. Some are born to sweet
delight but accord an eon for misery. Or so I sing, but

monody doesn't wake the machinists. Misericordia is ashbit.
Doesn't a ghost mean there's a bit the fire missed?

I keep at the box because—I am full of missing.

I see her face, form, dress. Who whispers *mercy*
and fans the flames? Miss stays so quiet, and this is

the mystery: who is wailing over the millwheel
Misericordia? *Misericordia*? A song strung of softest guts.

Corinna A-Maying the Apocalypse

It was a geologic instant.
Fine-bone plates moved under the Pawtuxet
& up sprang West Warwick. In an instant
the houses were up & the shutters open.
Then the paint was peeling all over town.
Then the instant passed with a shudder
& all the houses fell down.

The lilacs die. The lilies of the valley. April & May blow up & away.

"We are ready to live as before,"
says the last bald priest to the last white-May-dress girl,
who touches her chalked hopscotch sidewalk
& beneath her palm detects an earthquake
& in a gutter puddle sees her skull
& on her tongue catches a white blossom,
the last one. With her chalk she bawls
"The spring days are going to the graveyard."

The pet goat eats poison oak. The puppy bites the bitty lamb. All the kitty's whiskers fall away.

The little Lamb girl straddles a Chrysler Plymouth,
queen of the car parade, with a kitty
in her arm crook & a hand to the crowd.
She calls out, "I can see the end from here"
& tosses all West Warwick some Tootsie Rolls.
The Chrysler driver blows his horn.
Where have all the May-dress girls gone?
-To the classroom, for learning Latin & blushing
over Queen Dido's open, bebassing mouth.

The dust turns to tar. The rain to chalk. Undertakers cart snow angels away.

My hearse slides by a girl astride a puddle
wearing her mom's wedding gown. A downpour
smacks Arctic, Natick, the Greenwich Inn.
All the front door keys to all the places
I have ever lived drip from the dogwood tree
& chime in the wind. The girl in the gown
sinks. The puddle turns to a pond. West Warwick,
my West Warwick, drowns. Drowns world,
my clapboard castle & the moonface I was living in.

The Agonists

Norton Ave does not believe in tears. So the men's prison
overcrowds with crybabies, the grocery incinerates
all weptover produce & still the modest fathers
leap from their porches into traffic. All the sun
goes into their stovetops. Their corroded pennies
rub off losing jackpots. All their refrains start
Isn't That a Sad Story, & if he had all the ♥ on the block
& $, in all that anytime he never got any. Ask the old men
who leapt the railings into the puddles & fallgutters
how they get by. They look up the street & say
it's so lousy it's sublime. They look skyward, also questers
for God. In line at the Dunkin Donuts they believe
in the salt truck. In the How Will It End (on the tile
with his bootslush running off, on the tile with his coat
humming of last night's fish). If their lives move
quietly away from them they say this is just a flat stretch
of rain. There go the windshield wipers. Stop yourself
from putting a fist through the glass & you're a brave
man. Smash the windshield and it's Oh That Strong
Blood—your mom always said it'd get you. Don't ever
say what you want until you have it in hand.

Etymology for Clam Diggers

Break fathered *bless* like good intentions beget collisions, like Frank fathered
Vincent. I say this as Frank's barrels empty, as his clams clamber away

from the Mary Jos, the Michelin rubber, bay wrecks who gashed no scar on the surface water.
Because of blood, this bay's a viscous water to wade through. Because Frank's gut broke off

& crawled away to an earlier season, a better mud. To the bay, his innards were offered
& snapped up—leaving a bloody puddle he gives no investigation—his gut is broke,

here's the mark—he's always called the blood a blessing. Frank sifts through sand, says
when you're broke you're broke. You don't have a soaking dollar to bless yourself with.

Then he scrapes his knuckles against barnacles for blood, for stress. For the meanest of us,
broke means get used to your body breaking. As his mooring looses & the docks drink up the rot,

I hear *break* over & over—*bray, ache*—like a shriek. Frank takes it with a shrug & a *yes*.
No Sabatino ever screams while getting blessed.

Vincent's up next. Pioneering the last blesséd clamboat on the Sheepshead. *Blesséd*
in the colloquial—stubborn, stupid, there he goes loading his carcass onto the altar.

The struggle's to go back, scrute out the root: from a dock to a grove of scum & pilings,
from sea bed to a graveyard of the ferruginous Gillette & the Mary Jos jettisoned.

From *break* to *blessed with brine & blemish*.
To the grace of Vincent, the quahog-reeking son, receiving the broken boat

from his dad, the old Sabatino. Oh Frank, your gift's enough to heave-
ho, because what can Vinny do or save or halt if epic salt's his blessing—if his father insists

on quiet instead of dead, on not gone but (marked with blood) last week, last year, the everlasting.
On the dinghy, steady as water dripping, Vinny heaves through the dock groves. There he goes,

son of Frank, like grove is the child of greave. Greave—nothing he can do or bewail
but once a word for trees. Once in a while, I break my body to see my blood—*blessé*, the French

say for wounds. Italians have more guts—even if they're kaput—& say
suck it up. So bless the bloody bay. Bless the broken dock groves. Bless all Sabatinos.

Seven Generations of Stephen Bruneros

I, II, III, & IV

Bella, they all said, *bella bella*

but that came from the mouths of beermasters, milltown imperators
men not on any coin, who mowed laurels with weedwhacker scepters

The beautiful had zero to do with them

the septiemo Stephen Bruneros, who listed into lovely nothingness from the very first
Stephano, who conquered so many meatmarkets, all butchers named their firstborns Stephen—

Stephano Grocery Brunero.

Of whom one—pokerplayer, Rotary Club carddealer—left his debt to his son
(Guiltiamo) Stephen Brunero, who brought that to the dog track & often felt like

all the losing dogs were lying down

behind his breastbone—what his son S.B. would call *doghowl in the marrow.* No
not for me, S.B.'d yell to the dogs & like his grandfather, became a butcher to beat,

beat his malaise by pounding meat.

V

A man has a cat in his hands

& the sink is filling with water. Here begins a tender Palmolive bath for the cat
from the hands of Stephen Tiberius Brunero. Here begins, for many fine twilit seconds,

whimpering:

the cat, she's getting cold & oh, the poignancy is moist as the sink's
steam, as the fact of this man washing a cat after a day that began with him

sitting down on a dozen eggs.

In the awkwardness of tiny violences & the epic of small rooms, he's a colonel,
brunting each chore with yolk on his butt & *bella* between his lips, in a croon.

Curious how glorious

this ritual sink sluicing. The cat meeting her water bravely. Tragedy is flatly
saying *the day is cast*. This day is cast for the fifth, the sisyphusian Brunero,

& though we all may be fussy sissies

let us meet each other's eye tomorrow, going downhill, with finality, letting day be yolk
& night be butt & the Bruneros' grayish dishwater the best kind of perspicacity.

VI & VII

"Stevie Your Mine Scarface"

sprayed on the gas station wall by some girl: all we can know of #6 S. Brunero.
And that this smitten, smited girl mothered the seventh, who slept his life beneath a shelf

of Brunero bowling trophies

until a falling award broke his nose. How sad he was then, thinking of his mama hiding
all winter up a tree beside the gas station with a thermos of whiskey for his nose,

his stuffed-up Roman nose,

so he could nip between pumps & not lose his job. His mama up that tree
& all for his nose, his now-broken nose & now the dogs are off, howling in the marrow.

What can make it better

but to tell, of those winters, nips, the heaviness of that trophy, the who & who & who
& put the tree there, the gas pump there. We see the consolation in returning is

arriving, everyone has left the room.

VIII

A slight mythology of Brunero,

a Latin fortune in a Chinese cookie, *festina lente*, more haste, more haste & less
speed! oh Brunero, as you go through the motions of the eighth, ninth, tenth

Brunero, what a load

to have to be Stephano Brunero Continuous & yet lay down your load—there're a shitload
more Bruneros—fine flyspecks and small sagas, all—who went on and go on for kicks,

for kingpins & bourbon.

ETCETERA
(or, To Her Beloved Self, the Author Dedicates These Bruneros)

The beauty of the Bruneros trickles

not from facts exactly but from the facts piling their slough. The Bruneros eat a bigger hole
in the doghowling blight, rain though it may in the Brunero bedrooms—seven great leaky roofs

defying Corinthian & pedestrian dimensions.

But no, not for me. I will be suggesting no moral for this history. That I,
who watches the Brunero shoe-trudging lineage, can love the world, love it more

because of their pulchritudinous sadness.

Why should I want to feed with my youth the Bruneros' thin lips? Ahh, I like the largeness
of their sighs, expansive & buoyant as the dog track. (And if asked why the sigh, they say just—

That was my breath.)

For when I see the cat daily hurtling itself against the gas station wall I yell *Brunero,
Brunero*, & when I am old & finding my penny regrets glorious, I'll utter one *Brunero*,

other words not nearly tremendous.

Train Station Reincarnation

I was buying plastic bottles of water again
in our local supertank store

staring with the other shoppers at the water containers as if they were windows
into the pool or spring or pure silver faucet of their beginnings

when I felt that old exhilaration—
that old sense of space and people and a high ceiling.

I sat down on a shelf as if it were a shiny bench. Just how far from
our old train station was this place—material-wise?

The lost station with arcs and latticework and a moonstruck clock
that we carted off to the meadow, reduced to its parts.

Here, bowing over the produce division, could be the arcs
and in the shopping carts, I saw the latticework, and—

rows of water containers stood like rows of clerestory windows . . .

Yea, I proclaimed—*we have transitioned* train station *into a Titan's parts*:

Stain powder, spaghetti strainers, sanitation stock. Roast things, toast
things, tiaras, transistors. A few small nations. Tit for tat.

These crowds of parts—
assembled from the train station's swarms of folks—and the folks

were ghosts of the crowds of pre-station meadow grass . . . Perhaps
someone in the station missed the meadow beneath the tracks?

Not me. I *was* steering this toward a train station elegy, but for the tintinnabulation
calling me to Aisle Five, for a sale on rat-catchers and anti-nit ointment.

I was pushing my cart that way, and the others were pushing their carts
(we were the reverse of the linked cars that used to pull us)

when there, next to the sale items, I saw they had split *metropolis*,
left behind its slime and slop, and were selling its pools, and loops, and lipsticks.

And after saying to the stockboy, you repackage our train station
and you reparcel our metropolis—indignant, thinking of lost

tracks and arcs—   I stopped.

If you could have gotten a look at him—the stockboy—
he had stockboy boots, and probably dirty socks and yuks,

also a locomotive cap and sooty complexion and a Meadowlands concert t-shirt.
I felt that old sense of communion with him among the sale items.

I wanted to say to him, I don't know where to bear my loyalty.
But we were already aboard the ridiculous orb of this colossus—

and when the tintinnabulum sounded again and a voice requested artificial sod
assistance on Aisle Eleven, he went, and I followed him there.

four

Orienteering in the Land of the New Pirates

The New Pirates are men who, as infants,
told their moms *Keep your milk* and went and suckled gas pumps.

In towns of peril and experience, were the twelve-year olds
shrugging *It's an island all around and no water.*

Coming home to dark houses to moms saying, *Baby*
they turned our lights off.

ConEd turned their lights off. And ConEd turned
their stove off, turned their heat off. And Citgo
sucked the gas from their car. Citgo sucked back the gas from the car as they drove.

It wasn't that they weren't tender, didn't want to cry—
just, they saved up each yelp and lachrymal drop
till they could stick a finger in a socket and light up the house.

I am not the fountain of all pity.
We were afraid to go near that neighborhood.

I thought, with oiled tongues they will smile and kill.

Yes, I thought—and is this any better?—but when they do they are so beautiful.

Destiny for them is right now and right now and right now and the air with spit hovering in it.

Hiding in the town shadows, the air gagged
with electrical currents, the cars, the people on the street lagging—
even the moon lagging behind the tides—
they would come, the New Pirates, sparks in the dark.

And the light they make and the light they take is gold.

Some say they are a fairytale, yes, but if you could see the latest maps!

The world is all dark
except for the pulses of natural gas etched in purple
the white of fireflies and the golden coils that trace the movements of the New Pirates.

Plus the thin red light off one police car chasing them down.

If you flipped the switch on that map
you would have seen the little boys, New Pirates-at-the-ready,
standing in line like for a carnival ride

because isn't adventure always better than stagnant water?

—I say this standing waist deep in a swamp.

Sure the sludge this time of year is golden.
It is a swamp of ancient leaves, logs from ancient forests.
It is a few calendars until a seam of coal.

The golden sludge I think is a collection of sunlight.
It wants only to be stirred.

Once upon a time a crew of men robbed ships of the rich on the high rivers,
the highrises, the Hoover Dam.
Their treasure was energy, their loyalty to—living?

It sounds stupid.
We were afraid to even go near that neighborhood.

Still, if I had a son, I'd want him
to be a New Pirate. He'd be exhausted, always too thin, but that's an honest

heartbreak. I wouldn't want my boy to think the world is kind.
Wouldn't want him to think his games have no dark side.

The mothers in the tale were always supermarket braggarts—
My boy was the first to mechanize his fist.
My boy rides a windmill when he needs impetus.
blah blah blah, *he surfs on oil slicks.*

My boy says energy is the only life.

There goes my son, New Pirate Lawrence, spinning with an electric swarm of boys.
He doesn't leave me for the seas but for the black muck
of beaver dams and the light studs of unstable atoms—but for a spark.

And a spark to a small burn
or not. A spark to a small burn
or naught.

I imagine this waist deep in a swamp.

Or am I the swamp, wanting only to be stirred?

And who is the man on the map in the dark
eating out the heart of the swamp?

The New Constellation

I loved the Starbucks. I lived by the lip of the cup. I
lived at a slow clip and loved how the Starbucks sped
my blood. How the Starbucks spread its bucolic rug
and lit its electric fire—for any of us. And we stayed on
in the lamplight. We had our coffee and our milk.
Brown coffee and white sugar and a silvery
milk. It was all meant for us, in a way that the trees
and constellations were not. Our bills luminous,
our coins burnished. In the room of the Starbucks
what shone shone for us.
We did our work—I loved the white purpose.
The Starbucks hung no clock—I loved the silver sense
of time. No one knew me—all had a brown familiarity.
But soon soon I would be out on a tangled bank
as the river snarled and the night turned and the Starbucks shut . . .
To be sealed back inside!
I dreamt of a plastic energy, of the world set inside a box.
The box was a Starbucks where rivers turned to spigots,
the stars to satellites, and we all had a sterile bill or silver
cup of milk, trading one for the other, down the line,
across a broad path of brown rug . . . We shaped a worth
for the world. How I loved the made world. It afflicted me
how I loved the Starbucks. We had made it ourselves
with silvery hands. What a thing it was.

Song of the Tuxedo Rental Office

The tuxedoes stinking—of hotel bedspreads & aspirin dust.
Their legs spread open, whiffing,
they are done with standing straight up.

Of a Monday morning & its Saturday tuxes.
Steamhogs, the office girls, salesman Marv.

They make a roomlit rhythm
of things, things & things.
And the used tuxedoes writhe their polyester arms.

80 flits of the typing girl's hand
& a coat button's slow orbit around the floor.

The workers bend in the office wind.
The rhythm is so good sometimes.

The rhythm is so strong sometimes
it blows up the room.

The tuxedo office then a kind of weather,
a sky of small gestures.

The officegirls and steamhogs saved when blah Marv
calls, let's crawl inside a tent of manila folders.
Let's stitch a blanket of timecards to keep warm.

The rhythm now a windchime of paperclips & beyond that
from the showroom, the tuxedo footsteps, urgent.

Their pale message present
only like the sweat of someone lately gone—

what is it? who will ask?—and the fluorescents burn
the workers' shadows into waltz patterns on the wall.

The Last Entry in the Book of Blogs

The shepherdess held her head low as she asked me for paper. I have come down the mountain, she said, and her voice was not caught on the store's security tape. Her movements, her heavy garments were not caught by the electric eye. It was late, the store was closing, but she did not know how to read these signs. No moon that night. That week, per the almanac, nothing but cloudy and raining. It was the sort of hot night when the city had blackouts, the kind of electric weather the almanacs would eventually predict. No paper, but reams of memory on my computer.

The truth is, there were no mountains anywhere close—there were no sheep. But she had an ancient cane, and her robes were ample, and I thought *prophet* before *homeless*.

But I did not offer her my computer—it was the kind of night when letters on a screen didn't add up to words or symbols or even strung beads. And she moved with a mechanical stiffness, and I thought the paper might be for her last words, and if the power went off, her words would be nothing. A light suddenly turned off in the distance is at most light detritus— which is just blots . . . of darkness, in which the shepherdess wailed then, for parchment paper . . . *parchment oh parchment paper . . .*

It was then I thought we in cities should have kept some *things*.
To have slayed our lambs by the light of the moon then scrawled on their dried skins our last words—to have written on a house, or a rock, or on bark—
The moon is no longer the dish of silence that shepherds eat, or
Midnight's lambs had at least that bowl of moonmilk till morning.

In a kind of slow, slow nursery rhyme, the shepherdess shifted her wool tresses and lifted the veil from her face, revealing a beatific robot dying in the electronic night. *Long live this mystic science,* she said and turned to go.

Wait. I will email a message for you, I said.
Say, she said, *Where are you, moon?*

We waited. In that night of words, there was no habitable city for the mind. They said the natural moon was behind a cloud, but it was a wasted neon wreath called *moon*.

And no moon
had enough light waves left to wave its digits in goodbye.

We Will Meet Again on Other Pages

Subject: "DO YOU KNOW CHELSA????"
This is for all you hobos who live in abandoned castles—if you ever go online at
the public library, please read this—my sister is missing. Social Security says she
doesn't exist, but she did. Missing Persons says she may have burned in a fire on a
harbor estate, but no body was ever found. Someone has to stay home to comb
through the family ruin and that's me and my ruin is Chelsa, missing twenty-two
years, last seen in jeans and jelly shoes holding a stuffed dog, liked playing ring
around the rosy on the beach. At the market people always say whatever hap-
pened to Chelsa? Found a little summer boy & ran away with his family,
drowned swimming to the mainland, hoboing it up in an old harbor shack.
I want to slap their Nabisco treats right out of their hands. No shack—it's a
castle. Cas-ull. And she's dead, a parapet fell on her, smashed her like plaster,
like meringue into hundreds of dry white pieces. She's dead, a fire burned her
while she screamed in a turret and now she's hot, famous, salt-white ash or else
she lay in the lee of the castle and a fire spread through tall grasses to catch her
hair and now she's hot, famous, salt-white ash and your kids build sandcastles
with my sister. Here I am leading my little sister into flames and if you know
her please don't tell her this, but please write back.

Re: DO YOU KNOW CHELSA????
Maybe your sister was the girl I saw yesterday sleeping in a sandcastle's lee.

Re: DO YOU KNOW CHELSA????
Sorry. What I wrote was sort of a lie.
For you to think she was safe from wind, I said she slept in a lee.

Re: DO YOU KNOW CHELSA????
[removed]

Re: DO YOU KNOW CHELSA????
I keep seeing this singed woman singing ring around the rosy.
Her and you and me—out there with our bonfires on the black water.

The New Song of Songs

There were sixty queens, eighty concubines, and virgins without number:
Madison eating strudel in her skivvies and Mom reroping her bathrobe,
Aunt Jen meddling and Mackenzie gum-smacking and in the corner the cousins,
all with diet juice, breakfasting. But Missy the darling, in her baby chair,
legs dangling, sang *I make love to my boyfriend.* And Mom said *let's discuss
how Missy has no breasts* and Missy sang *I sex my boyfriend* and Mom said
she has no breasts yet and what will we do tomorrow, the day she is spoken for?
And our pooch howled like a beast and Missy gazed towards her bedroom,
singing *I charge you, O my sisters, do not wake up my boyfriend.*
And we loved the way she talked. She was like a dark book in a green night
and we were in a bright kitchen. The door was the door and the window
the window and nothing had a secret meaning. But for Missy who sang
he kisses me with the kisses of his mouth.
And then Mom laid her own bra in Missy's lap. And we loved our sister,
so we took our silk scarves and lined up, grim as an army with banners,
and we filled the bra and we called her *fairest among women.*
And Missy sang *my breasts are towers and my boyfriend will climb them.*
And our white paint turned to dark wood and our floors to deep wells
and Mom, who had been so strong, said *how soon breakfast gives way to feast,
how soon our rooms fall to wrecks, how softly my baby takes her sentence!*
. . . Then all of us wanted a wedding too. We wanted a feeling dark
and old-fashioned, but real, real and in the room. And Missy with her breasts
like two ancient fallen towers, her winter past, her rain over and gone,
opened her bedroom door and sang *go forth, O my sisters, behold my boyfriend.*

Sit on a Potato Pan, Otis

It is such a rainy day I had to write you
from my potato pan to prove I really do exist—
it's just long ago I stuck my head in the sand.
Ostracized by ostriches, I made friends with tubers.
I guess the dirt is lovely this time of year.
But make me an offer
of your pity laced with phlegm, and you will have
my belly as a pillow for one exquisite afternoon.
In earnest,
Otis, The Guy Who Sells Trinkets at the Mall

I was buying sunglasses from him as he wrote this missive
and begged to mail it on his behalf, which I did. Did I
first peruse the envelope? Yes—and when my eye saw this address—
To We Few of the Dirt—I prayed that the Dead Letter Office
would take his SOS and burn it , so that the ash, raining to earth
at noon, would be eaten by the worms, his dirt brethren.
Fire blazes the best path to the dead, to the forlorn solos—
let no tuber rebut. And Otis letters by the cartload get gutted,
mercifully, mercifully.
Yet, later, while kayaking with a postal inspector,
I was informed that the deified Dead Letter Office was dead.
To whom can the reviled deliver themselves now?
All the mail is posted and gone and there is so much letter left.

Dear Otis, if only your dispatch could reach Sito, the ice cream man
who all day long pushes his ghostcart under the radar,
Sito, who walks a line in circles then walks his dud cart back again . . .
but O pale man, my dad, my little boy, what post office
will receive you, who's drawn inward enough to carry you there?

Department of Tenderness

To my dear Monsieur Denert, re: your intent
to turn the Dept. of Defense into one of Tenderness:

I assent—we have all been teens or nerds—
so really no one's our enemy, really
every Ted, Ned and Nettie should tend to one another
for who hasn't at least ten needs
who hasn't netted a few dents or wouldn't
tender next month's rent to be nuzzled by a deer?
Yet I cannot house your Department in me.
See, I have feeling for this stern monsieur
who has made me tenders of his gentleness
but he will not caress me until he offends
me—this trend's implicit in tenderness
and *I* at least comprehend the skeletons
who will finger my dress when I demand it.
Your Dept. will be fenced in skin from girls' wrists
and passersby will need to slit it, for tenderness
portends an Eden for the violent. Don't pretend
tenderness waits on all—its tendons stretch
only to smooth over its last vehement gesture,
for what's more tender than the hand that slaps me?
It's rendered, then rent, then cleft
under pretend names like "Dept. of Tenderness,"
the casements of which I will peer inside
on tender weather days, holding my monsieur's
red hand, yearning for tenderness, calling
through your halls for tenderness in a voice
tenuous as yellow and you will sneer in return,
"It has departed. Get a different word."

Interior Ghazal of a Lousy Girl

I am the excess of exuberance,
one crummy girl swallowing ruin—all the sweet
pork pies, all the Rumford Mill pudding.
Rumford, where I cry from lawn sprinklers,
where I shovel myself into ice puddles,
where the Rumford dog waits daylong for a hug—
and on I walk.
Rumford is full of the cats I have jammed my foot into.
I should stop it now, stop it and begin a lusty recovery.
Like how my brother professes wetly on paper doilies.
I have no room to do.
Things are peanut butter in my stomach,
things are Peter Peter Pumpkin Eater
in my gullet. Now I open it up—
I'm lousy in deed & episode
I'm lousy with desire & Rumford.
The cats sit in kingdom come
with all the Rumford hamsters & all the Rumford nuns.
Shit, sorry, I should whistle a lovely recovery.
Like how my brother professes tenderly in faxed testimonies.
Can do—can do—this girl says the borscht can do.
So, to a pastoral:
Me down by the Mobil Mart with some peanut butter cups.
An island of peat moss, a grove of air hoses,
scraps of bitten chiclets, vomit, & the wind
through the gas pumps bearing my chatter.
Behind a Honda an iceberg drum kicks up:

> *Kingdom come.*
> *Bring rum. Come.*
>
> *Sling, strum, come.*
> *Stinging crumb, come.*

Denning mum. Come,
my sobbing plum, come.

Have you seen the girl with her thumb in the Rumford dam?
Or the old woman who lived in a slue?
Boo-hoo, boo-hoo, goes my sobbing Rumford plum.
I would undo what I've undone.

Bullet

It was like a heavy seed, so I thought, Plant it.
No soil so I swallowed it.

How to make it not the thrown stone, not the grape of wrath.
Make it not the animal's eye gleaming at the attack.

Think tuft of cotton not glint of cobalt.
A bluebell in my woods near moss.

There will be a loud report.
No. There will be snow falling on the shrub.

It was a heart and I its house and I opened my door and it went out.

Small button on a blouse, then buckle of a belt.
But there was its pulse.

The tip of a jackhammer, tongue of an alarm.
I sang along.

I looked right in the mother's gleaming eye.
It's innocent, I said. Innocent.

Small ball.
No. I swear when my fingers unfurled I held—a silver jonquil.

Maybe I mothered when I should have fathered.
Maybe a seed not for the start but for the end.

There was a small ball in the boy's fist. And a voice in his ear, *Throw it.*